MICHAEL TODD

Crazy Faith

IT'S ONLY CRAZY UNTIL IT HAPPENS.

STUDY GUIDE | FIVE SESSIONS

Harper*Christian*
Resources

𝕮𝖗𝖆𝖟𝖞 𝕱𝖆𝖎𝖙𝖍 Study Guide
© 2022 by Michael Todd

Requests for information should be addressed to:
HarperChristian Resources, 3900 Sparks Dr. SE, Grand Rapids, Michigan 49546

ISBN 978-0-310-15932-2 (softcover)
ISBN 978-0-310-15933-9 (ebook)

All Scripture quotations are taken from The Holy Bible, New International Version®, NIV®. Copyright © 1973, 1978, 1984, 2011 by Biblica, Inc.™ Used by permission. All rights reserved worldwide.

Any internet addresses (websites, blogs, etc.) and telephone numbers in this study guide are offered as a resource. They are not intended in any way to be or imply an endorsement by HarperChristian Resources, nor does HarperChristian Resources vouch for the content of these sites and numbers for the life of this study guide.

HarperChristian Resources titles may be purchased in bulk for church, business, fundraising, or ministry use. For information, please e-mail ResourceSpecialist@ ChurchSource.com.

Published in association with The Bindery Agency, www.TheBinderyAgency.com.

First Printing July 2022 / Printed in the United States of America

CONTENTS

INTRODUCTION

"That's crazy!" "Don't be crazy." "You're crazy."

I'm sure we've all made statements like these in the past. Most of the time, we're not implying the person we're talking with is *actually* crazy. (Emphasis on "most.") Rather, we use the word to show we're feeling a bit uncomfortable about the situation or the topic of discussion. We're concerned the person we're addressing has stepped too far away from what we would consider *normal*, and we want them to come back a little closer to reality.

Well, buckle up, because it's actually my hope that this study will make you feel a little uncomfortable—or maybe even a *lot* uncomfortable. I'm going to ask you to forget what you've always thought about spiritual reality. And I'm definitely going to push you to stay far away from what many Christians believe to be *normal* when it comes to matters of faith.

I'm going to ask you to get a little *crazy*.

Over the course of this study, you and I are going to work together to wrap our minds around a way of thinking and doing that I call 𝕮𝖗𝖆𝖟𝖞 𝕱𝖆𝖎𝖙𝖍. This is the kind of faith we see demonstrated on every page of our Bibles. The kind of faith that gets a person to walk on the water. The kind of faith that places the fate of an army into the palm of an old man's hand. The kind of faith that raises the dead.

That's 𝕮𝖗𝖆𝖟𝖞 𝕱𝖆𝖎𝖙𝖍.

Are you feeling a little nervous? Even a little freaked out? Trust me, that's good. After all, when you think about it, when has anyone accomplished anything worthwhile when they were consistently comfortable and complacent in their normal, non-crazy lives?

You and I want something bigger. We want the abundant life that Jesus promised to all who follow him. We want to experience meaning, purpose, fulfillment, and joy.

Are you ready to grab those dreams? Good. Let's get a little crazy.

— MICHAEL TODD

HOW TO USE THIS GUIDE

The **Crazy Faith** video study is designed to be experienced both in group settings (such as a Bible study, Sunday school class, or small group gatherings) as well as in your individual study time. Each session, which covers material from two chapters in the book, begins with an introduction, two questions to inspire thought about the topic, and brief passages from the Bible. You will then watch a video featuring Michael Todd, which is available via streaming and can be accessed using the instructions on the inside front cover.

If you are doing this study with a group, you will be prompted to engage in targeted discussions and close with a time of personal reflection and prayer. Each person in the group should have his or her own copy of this study guide, and you are also encouraged to have a copy of the **Crazy Faith** book, as reading it alongside the curriculum will provide you with deeper insights. The "For Next Session" section details the chapters in the book that correspond to the material you will be discussing during your next group time.

To get the most out of your group experience, keep the following points in mind:

1. **The real growth in this study will happen during your small-group time.** This is where you will process the teaching content of the session, ask

questions, and learn from others as you hear what God is doing in their lives. For this reason, be fully committed to the group and attend each session so you can build trust and rapport with the other members. Your decision to go "all in" will increase your chances of getting more out of this study.

2. **The goal of your small group is to serve as a place where people can share, learn about God, and build intimacy and friendship.** Seek to make your group a safe place, which means being honest about your thoughts and feelings and listening to everyone else's opinion. (If you are a group leader, there are additional instructions in the back for leading a productive discussion group.)

3. **Resist the temptation to fix a problem someone might be having or correct his or her theology.** Also, keep everything your group shares confidential. This will foster a rewarding sense of community in your group and create a place where people can heal, be challenged, and grow spiritually.

Following your group time, you can reflect on the material that you've covered by engaging in the between-sessions activities. For each session, you may wish to complete the personal study all in one sitting or spread it out over a few days. If you are unable to start or finish your between-sessions personal study, you are still welcome to attend the group time. You'll never be excluded from the group, even if you don't have your "homework" done.

Remember, the videos, discussion questions, and activities are simply meant to kick-start your imagination. They will help you to be open to what God wants you to hear and how he wants you to apply it. As you go through this study, listen to what he is saying to you and consider your own journey in light of what you learn about living in 𝕮𝖗𝖆𝖟𝖞 𝕱𝖆𝖎𝖙𝖍.

Sound good? Then let's get started!

SESSION 1
STARTING OUT
(BABY FAITH AND MAYBE FAITH)

CHAPTER 2   CHAPTER 3

Everything is possible for one who believes.

MARK 9:23

WELCOME

As I write these words, scientists at NASA are working on a three-month plan to align eighteen different hexagonal mirrors that make up the James Webb Space Telescope. It's an ambitious project. In fact, it's the kind of project that many people would call crazy.

One of the things that makes the James Webb Space Telescope so impressive is its location. While the familiar Hubble Telescope takes pictures from orbit around our own planet, the James Webb Space Telescope is in orbit around the sun. In fact, it's out there doing its thing all by itself in deep space—more than a million miles away from the earth. Something else that sets the telescope apart is its heat shield. The telescope's delicate instruments are designed to pick up the smallest heat or infrared signature out in the farthest reaches of the universe. For that reason, it has to be kept incredibly cold . . . which is a problem because it is directly exposed to the rays of the sun.

So, scientists constructed a heat shield on the back of the telescope to block out that solar energy. As NASA has said, "The temperature difference between the hot and cold sides of the telescope is huge. You could almost boil water on the hot side, and you could freeze nitrogen on the cold side!"[1]

Once it is fully operational, the telescope will be able to look pretty much anywhere in the vast expanse of space—including the dust-filled heart of nebulae where new exoplanets are forming. The telescope's highly specialized instruments will also be on the lookout for water and other signs of life currently hidden among distant solar systems. And the telescope might even be able to assist in dating the age of stars.[2]

Now, it's crazy to think about a group of scientists here on earth accessing such a complicated telescope from a million ·

miles away—and then using it to seek out answers to our biggest questions about space and life and what might exist in this universe other than ourselves. Yet it's happening. Right now. Right this moment.

But of course . . . it didn't happen *overnight*. The plans that led to the James Webb Telescope didn't materialize out of thin air. They were not the product of anyone's spontaneous idea. Rather, scientists took baby steps and set small goals to reach their larger crazy goals. They didn't always have the information they needed to guarantee their next step would lead to success. Sometimes, they had to take "maybe" steps.

We're going to take the same approach when it comes to learning about Crazy Faith. In this session, we're starting where the scientists did by exploring the important steps of baby faith and maybe faith. In other words, we're going to start small together before we go big.

SHARE

If you or any of your group members are just getting to know one another, take a few minutes to introduce yourselves. Then, to kick things off, discuss one of the following questions:

- When have you seen something happen in your life or reached a goal that at first you thought was too crazy to achieve?

— *or* —

- What is the first thing that comes to your mind when you think about the concept of faith?

READ

Invite someone to read aloud the following passage. Listen for fresh insights as you hear the verses being read, and then discuss the questions that follow.

> *Now faith is confidence in what we hope for and assurance about what we do not see. This is what the ancients were commended for. By faith we understand that the universe was formed at God's command, so that what is seen was not made out of what was visible.*

> HEBREWS 11:1-3

How does this passage add to your understanding of what faith is and why it's important?

What are some ways that each of us demonstrate faith in our everyday lives?

WATCH

Watch the video segment for session one. (Play the DVD or see the instructions on the inside front cover on how to access the sessions through streaming.) As you and your group watch, use the following outline to record any thoughts or concepts that stand out to you.

God wants you to have **Crazy Faith**—to not just be one who sits on the sidelines but who steps out in **Crazy Faith**, against all odds, and does what may not make complete sense but will make a miracle.

The faith journey starts with baby faith. Now, most of us don't like to do anything small. But the truth is that baby faith is perhaps the most important step in starting your journey of faith.

Your imagination unlocked could start a **Crazy Faith** journey that will change your family, your ideas, and who you are and how you impact others forever. Unlocking your imagination is the beginning of taking baby steps of faith.

A mustard seed is one of the smallest seeds in the world. But God says with that little bit of small faith, you can have mountain-moving faith. So take a baby step and see what God can do with something small.

God is trying to get you out of your comfort zone into what could be called the "gray zone," "crazy zone," or—most commonly known to people of 𝕮𝖗𝖆𝖟𝖞 𝕱𝖆𝖎𝖙𝖍—the "grace zone." This journey you are on has some maybes attached to it. You will not always be 100% sure of what will happen if you make a move, but all you need is 51% to take that first step.

You don't have to understand everything to be obedient. You can step out in maybe faith. Faith begins where understanding ends. It may not always make sense to you, but it can always make a miracle.

Here is the faith formula: "intellectual agreement + trust = faith." Intellectual agreement is the knowledge that something is true as acquired through teaching and experience. Trust, however, is reliance on what you know is true. Unless you have both . . . you don't have faith.

Everything you want to see in your life can happen as you step out in baby faith and maybe faith. So don't stop now! Keep moving forward and allow God to show you who you can be. He knows exactly what is best for you, and he knows what you need.

DISCUSS

As you consider what you just watched, use the following questions to discuss these ideas, their basis in Scripture, and their application in your life with your group members.

1. Think about the statement, "It's only crazy until it happens." What are some examples from your life that support that claim? When has God called you to do something crazy?

2. Read Ephesians 3:14–21. What would you like God to accomplish in your life that is "immeasurably more" than you feel comfortable asking or imagining?

3. **Crazy Faith** is "having thoughts and actions that lack reason but trusting fully in what you cannot explicitly prove." Who have you seen demonstrate that kind of faith?

4. How would you summarize the concept of baby faith? What are some baby steps of faith that you have taken in the past few months?

5. How would you summarize the concept of maybe faith? When are times you stepped out in faith even though you were not 100% sure of the outcome?

6. Read Genesis 12:1–9. What are some ways that Abram demonstrated the different kinds of faith that we have discussed in this session?

RESPOND

Briefly review the outline for the video teaching and any notes you took. Write down your responses to these two questions: (1) What can I do this week that would show baby faith? (2) What can I do this week that would show maybe faith?

PRAY

One of the most important things you can do together in community is to pray for one another. This is not simply a closing prayer to end your group time but a portion of time to share prayer requests, review how God has answered past prayers, and actually pray for one another. So, as you close your time together, thank God for his gift of faith—for the gift of being able to act and trust him enough to move forward even when you don't have everything figured out. Express your desire to act in baby faith and maybe faith. Finally, use the space below to write down any specific prayer requests or praises that you have for the group.

Name   **Request/Praise**

PERSONAL STUDY

You are on a journey toward living out **Crazy Faith** in your everyday life. But you won't be making that journey in one leap! Growing in **Crazy Faith** starts with baby faith and maybe faith. And a key part of that growth, regardless of where you are spiritually, involves studying God's Word. This is the goal of these personal studies—to help you explore what the Bible has to say about faith and how to apply it to your life. For this opening session, you may want to begin by reviewing chapters 1–3 in **Crazy Faith**. As you work through this content, be sure to read the reflection questions and make a few notes in your guide about the experience. At the start of the next session, you will have a few minutes to share any insights you learned.

A PICTURE OF BABY FAITH

It must have been a truly chaotic scene. If you were to stumble across that moment in history, the first thing you would notice is the boy—the demon-possessed boy. Picture him there on the ground, rolling around and frothing at the mouth. He has no control over his own body.

Right above the boy—with a terrified look on his face and hands stretched out in a gesture of protection—is his father. Surrounding those two are nine out of Jesus' disciples. Out beyond the disciples, always watching and waiting to see what will happen next, is the crowd.

You have to feel sorry for Jesus' disciples in that moment. It's clear they wanted to help. They had likely spent hours in a spiritual battle against the demonic forces at play. They had prayed. They had claimed the name of Jesus. They had laid their hands on the child and done everything they could think of to free him from the torment of the demon.

But it wasn't working. Not at all. And everyone around was watching them fail.

But then came the miracle. Jesus appeared on the scene, trailed by Peter and James and John. The disciples probably saw him making his way down the mountain, and you can just picture them gesturing frantically for him to come and help. "Lord! Master! Over here, please!"

Let's have Mark take it from here:

> "You unbelieving generation," Jesus replied, "how long shall I stay with you? How long shall I put up with you? Bring the boy to me."
>
> So they brought him. When the spirit saw Jesus, it immediately threw the boy into a convulsion. He fell to the ground and rolled around, foaming at the mouth.
>
> Jesus asked the boy's father, "How long has he been like this?"

"From childhood," he answered. "It has often thrown him into fire or water to kill him. But if you can do anything, take pity on us and help us."

" 'If you can'?" said Jesus. "Everything is possible for one who believes."

Immediately the boy's father exclaimed, "I do believe; help me overcome my unbelief!"

When Jesus saw that a crowd was running to the scene, he rebuked the impure spirit. "You deaf and mute spirit," he said, "I command you, come out of him and never enter him again."

The spirit shrieked, convulsed him violently and came out. The boy looked so much like a corpse that many said, "He's dead." But Jesus took him by the hand and lifted him to his feet, and he stood up.

MARK 9:19-27

Notice that moment between Jesus and the boy's father. "But if you can do anything, take pity on us and help us." Jesus noticed that littlest of words: "if." It's a word filled with doubt, and Jesus was quick to call it out. "Everything is possible for one who believes."

Now back to the father. He's just been rebuked—corrected in public—by Jesus the Miracle Worker. He is the one whom some are saying could actually be the Messiah. But the father didn't pay that rebuke any mind. The only thing he cared about was his son rolling on the ground beneath him. "I do believe," the father cried out. "Help me overcome my unbelief!"

Now, *that's* baby faith. A little step in the right direction. The father was saying, "Lord, I don't have what it takes to heal my son, and I just admitted that I'm not sure if you can heal him either. But please help me remove that fear and doubt.

Please help me get over this uncertainty. Please help me have the kind of faith that I need to see my boy become well."

Can you pray that kind of prayer today? "Lord, help me take a little step closer to you." If so, you already have everything you need to walk in baby faith as a follower of Christ.

In what ways do you relate to the father of the boy in this story?

What are some obstacles that consistently get in the way of your ability to believe that "everything is possible" with God?

What is one step that you could take to start to remove those obstacles?

A PICTURE OF MAYBE FAITH

There's no doubt that Joshua has to be considered one of the baddest dudes in the Bible. He was a skilled warrior. He was a born leader who had been mentored by Moses himself. And he had just been appointed to direct the armies of God's chosen people, the Israelites.

Still, even Joshua had to be scratching his head when he looked up at the walls of Jericho. They were *huge* walls. Big enough to have rooms and apartments set into the stone. And yet, somehow, Joshua was supposed to knock them down. Now, he was probably thinking "somehow," though the instructions he had received from God were clear enough:

> *"See, I have delivered Jericho into your hands, along with its king and its fighting men. March around the city once with all the armed men. Do this for six days. Have seven priests carry trumpets of rams' horns in front of the ark. On the seventh day, march around the city seven times, with the priests blowing the trumpets. When you hear them sound a long blast on the trumpets, have the whole army give a loud shout; then the wall of the city will collapse and the army will go up, everyone straight in."*
>
> Joshua 6:2–5

Yes, the instructions were clear . . . but it wasn't clear how something as silly as marching around the city could knock down stone walls. You can almost see the other generals stopping by Joshua's tent for a little chat. "Hey, Josh, are you sure this is going to work?"

Here's the reality: Joshua *wasn't* sure. He *wasn't* certain. The Bible doesn't say that, but we can go out on a limb here and say there is no way that Joshua felt 100% convinced that gathering Israel's army and marching around the walls of Jericho was really and truly enough to cause those walls to fall. Maybe he felt 67% sure. Or maybe it was closer to 51%. Regardless, he had the courage to take God at his word, even though he didn't fully understand how God planned to come through and fulfill His promises.

In other words, Joshua operated in maybe faith. He obeyed God and led that march. Here's what happened next:

> *On the seventh day, they got up at daybreak and marched around the city seven times in the same manner, except that on that day they circled the city seven times. The seventh time around, when the priests sounded the trumpet blast, Joshua commanded the army, "Shout! For the LORD has given you the city! The city and all that is in it are to be devoted to the LORD. Only Rahab the prostitute and all who are with her in her house shall be spared, because she hid the spies we sent. . . ." When the trumpets sounded, the army shouted, and at the sound of the trumpet, when the men gave a loud shout, the wall collapsed; so everyone charged straight in, and they took the city.*
>
> JOSHUA 6:15–17, 20

What stands out the most to you about Joshua's actions in this story? Why?

Try to put yourself in the shoes of one of Israel's soldiers. What emotions would you have experienced during that final march? What questions would have been in your mind?

What does this story reveal about the power of acting in maybe faith?

WALKING IN Crazy Faith

Have you ever tried to return something at a store but then realized that you forgot the receipt? Most retailers won't take returns if you can't present a receipt as proof that you actually purchased an item. If you're attempting to return something expensive from a high-end department store and don't have a receipt, the experience can get even more awkward.

A receipt is evidence that a transaction has occurred. But when it comes to your faith, God accepts *invisible* evidence. Imagine for a moment that God is the owner of the highest-end department store in your city. You walk in to purchase a few items, and when you go to the counter to check out, the clerk tells you that someone has already paid for everything. All you have to do is show your receipt to leave the store with the items you've chosen.

What is that receipt? It's simply your faith—trusting in something that you cannot explicitly prove. Faith is your receipt . . . your invisible evidence that you can claim those items that God said you could take. You can't see it, but you can believe it. You can believe for things that seem impossible, things that are currently intangible, things that are so big that they seem immeasurable. God simply requires you to have faith for him to take care of the end result.

Faith is having confidence in who God is—and he responds to that kind of confidence! After all, what father doesn't like when his kids brag about him? Even a small amount of confidence opens the door for you to begin believing that God can and will do even greater good for you, in you, and through you.

The Bible states, "Faith is confidence in what we hope for and assurance about what we do not see" (Hebrews 11:1). When you come to understand the authority that has been given to you as a believer in Christ, you begin to pray with a level of faith that brings about assurance. Not *insurance* . . . but *assurance*. Insurance is something you pay into to restore assets or supplement income in the event that you experience a loss. It can't always restore everything that has been damaged, and it gives back to you only according to what you put into it.

Assurance, however, is a reliable truth outside yourself on which you can confidently depend. It's already purchased and is freely given to you.[3]

When have you had an experience that you were certain was connected to faith—a moment when you knew you were demonstrating faith?

What reasons do you have for feeling confident in God?

When have you seen God respond to your level of confidence in him?

For Next Session: Write down any insights or questions you want to discuss at the next group meeting. In preparation for the next session, review chapters 4 and 5 in 𝕮𝖗𝖆𝖟𝖞 𝕱𝖆𝖎𝖙𝖍.

SESSION 2
GETTING STRONGER
(WAITING FAITH AND WAVY FAITH)
CHAPTER 4   CHAPTER 5

Be strong and courageous. Do not be afraid;
do not be discouraged,
for the LORD your God will be with you.

JOSHUA 1:9

WELCOME

Over the past ten years, Brian Shaw has four times been awarded the title of "World's Strongest Man." Actually, *awarded* is the wrong word. Mr. Shaw *earned* that title four times by competing in a grueling series of challenges at the World's Strongest Man annual competition. If you're not familiar with that competition, think of it as the Olympics for Schwarzeneggers.

One of the events is called the Vehicle Pull. Competitors wear a specialized harness attached to a set of ropes. Those ropes are then attached to a huge vehicle of some kind. Sometimes, it's a train car. Other times, it's an airplane or a bus. When everything is hooked up, the athletes heave, tug, and pull that vehicle 100 feet to the finish line. The fastest time wins.

That's just one event. There is also the Hercules Hold, which requires athletes to stand between two 350-pound pillars, grab hold of two chains, and try and prevent those pillars from falling down for as long as they can. But the most famous event is probably the Atlas Stones. This event features five spherical boulders, each one weighing between 220 and 350 pounds. The athletes have to pick up those boulders off the ground, one at a time, and heave them up onto the top of elevated pillars. The one who heaves the fastest is the winner.[4]

Yeah, it's crazy. And we can assume that the men who voluntarily train for and compete in the World's Strongest Man competition are probably a little bit crazy themselves. But there is a principle that we can gain from their example: *it takes work to get stronger.*

This is certainly true of physical strength. But it's also true when it comes to our faith. As we saw in the previous session, we don't go from no faith to 𝕮𝖗𝖆𝖟𝖞 𝕱𝖆𝖎𝖙𝖍 in the space of a day. It takes a little training. It takes a little perseverance. It can take a *lot* of waiting. And sometimes . . . it can take some willingness on our part to step away from what is safe.

Now that you're familiar with baby faith and maybe faith, we're going to get a little stronger in this session by exploring waiting faith and wavy faith. Let's get to work!

SHARE

If you or any of your group members are just getting to know one another, take a few minutes to introduce yourselves and share any insights you have from your personal study. Then, to kick things off, discuss one of the following questions:

- How do you typically handle waiting? Do you consider yourself more of a patient or impatient person? Explain.

— or —

- What is a goal that you set for yourself in the past that required you to work hard over a long period of time to achieve?

READ

Invite someone to read aloud the following passage. Listen for fresh insights as you hear the verses being read, and then discuss the questions that follow.

> *Do you not know that in a race all the runners run, but only one gets the prize? Run in such a way as to get the prize. Everyone who competes in the games goes into strict training.*

They do it to get a crown that will not last, but we do it to get a crown that will last forever. Therefore I do not run like someone running aimlessly; I do not fight like a boxer beating the air. No, I strike a blow to my body and make it my slave so that after I have preached to others, I myself will not be disqualified for the prize.

1 CORINTHIANS 9:24–27

What is the *prize* that all followers of Jesus are working and training to achieve?

What are some ways you are hoping to grow or develop when it comes to your faith?

WATCH

Watch the video segment for session two. (Play the DVD or see the instructions on the inside front cover on how to access the sessions through streaming.) As you and your group watch, use the following outline to record any thoughts or concepts that stand out to you.

We live in a fast-paced world. We want to see results *now*. But patience and perseverance have tremendous value in the kingdom of God and are essential on this journey of **Crazy Faith**.

The gap between what you're believing for and when it actually happens is often on purpose. God is preparing you for the promise that he has in store for you. Your character needs to be prepared.

Saul's impatience cost him the entire kingdom. In this season where things seem unstable and it looks like you could just make things happen . . . where is your wait? *Will* you wait on God? Because the only thing worse than waiting on God is wishing that you had.

When you start serving in the wait, it changes your perspective on the wait. In the midst of whatever situation you're believing God to show up in in **Cra3y Jaith**, don't just act in baby faith or maybe faith . . . but actually live and love and lead in waiting faith.

Spend some time in God's Word, and you'll notice the Bible doesn't highlight stories of people who play it safe, stay at home, and stay comfortable. We rarely talk about people who stay safe and dry in the boat. No, we talk about people who trust Jesus enough to get their feet wet and walk on the water.

Jesus' invitation to come to him on the water was an open invitation for all the disciples to step out in **Cra3y Jaith**. But only Peter had the audacity. Only he had the **Cra3y Jaith** to make that move. Could it have been that God wanted all twelve of the disciples to walk on water that day?

God wants to encourage you through Peter's story to walk in wavy faith. Stepping out of the boat was the *safest* place Peter could be, because Jesus was there. If the Savior is there, you're safe.

It's not our job to save ourselves. It's our job to trust completely in the Savior of the world and get close to him. Walking with the Savior requires us to step out of what it's safe.

DISCUSS

As you consider what you just watched, use the following questions to discuss these ideas, their basis in Scripture, and their application in your life with your group members.

1. Perseverance and patience are two keys for getting stronger in your faith. Who has modeled those values in your life? How did they model those traits?

2. How would you describe what it means to exercise waiting faith?

3. Read 1 Samuel 13:1–15. What reasons did King Saul have for disobeying God's command in that moment? What reasons did he have for obeying?

4. How would you describe what it means to exercise wavy faith?

5. Read Matthew 14:22–36. What are some of the ways that your spiritual life and spiritual growth have been negatively impacted by fear?

6. What are some of the biggest obstacles that prevent followers of Jesus from developing waiting faith in their lives?
What about wavy faith?

RESPOND

Briefly review the outline for the video teaching and any notes
you took. Write down your responses to these two questions:
(1) What can I do this week that would show waiting faith?
(2) What can I do this week that would show wavy faith?

PRAY

As you close your time together, confess that God's timetable is always best and ask him to give you patience to wait on his timing. Pray that he will give you wisdom to know when it's time to step out in faith—even in the midst of a storm. Use the space below to record any specific prayer requests or praises that you have for the group.

Name　　　　　　　　**Request/Praise**

PERSONAL STUDY

Reflect on the material you covered during the group time by engaging in any or all of the following between-session activities. Be sure to read the reflection questions and make a few notes in your guide about the experience. At the start of your next group session, you will have a few minutes to share any insights that you learned.

A PICTURE OF WAITING FAITH

Thirty-eight years is a long time. Take a moment to think about what you were doing thirty-eight years ago. What were the biggest dreams or motivations in your life? Maybe you were just out of college and ready to conquer the world. Maybe you were feeling thankful just to be out of high school. Maybe thirty-eight years ago you were just out of diapers. Or maybe . . . you can't think back to thirty-eight years ago because you hadn't been born yet.

Thirty-eight years ago, the biggest songs on the radio were "Jump" by Van Halen, "When Doves Cry" by Prince, and "Smooth Operator" by Sade. The biggest movies at the box office were *Ghostbusters*, *Gremlins*, and *Indiana Jones and the Temple of Doom*. Thirty-eight years ago, the Raiders won the Super Bowl, the Celtics won the NBA championship, and the Detroit Tigers won the World Series.[5]

Okay, by now you're probably thinking, *What's with this obsession about everything that happened thirty-eight years ago?* The answer to that question is a story from Scripture:

> *Some time later, Jesus went up to Jerusalem for one of the Jewish festivals. Now there is in Jerusalem near the Sheep Gate a pool, which in Aramaic is called Bethesda and which is surrounded by five covered colonnades. Here a great number of disabled people used to lie—the blind, the lame, the paralyzed. One who was there had been an invalid for thirty-eight years. When Jesus saw him lying there and learned that he had been in this condition for a long time, he asked him, "Do you want to get well?"*
>
> *"Sir," the invalid replied, "I have no one to help me into the pool when the water is stirred. While I am trying to get in, someone else goes down ahead of me."*
>
> *Then Jesus said to him, "Get up! Pick up your mat and walk." At once the man was cured; he picked up his mat and walked.*
>
> JOHN 5:1–9

The man in this story had been disabled for *thirty-eight years*. Almost four entire decades of tugging on useless legs, crawling on scabbed elbows, and begging for help. It had to be exhausting. Yet there's something inspiring about this man: *he hadn't given up.*

There was a legend in Jerusalem that whenever the waters were stirred at the pool of Bethesda, the first person to enter would be healed. That's where Jesus found this man. At the pool, doing everything he could to get into the water. But really, what he was doing was waiting. Waiting for God to do something—*anything*—to improve his situation.

Hopefully, you will never have to wait thirty-eight years for God to accomplish a dream or fulfill a promise in your life. But you *will* wait. That's a given. So, it's critical that you learn how to wait in faith. It's essential that you learn how to believe God is good and to believe that He has a purpose even when you don't understand it. Even when it's been months—or years.

Here's the truth. When you learn to wait in faith in God's timing, even those long seasons of waiting can become times of increased intimacy, connection, trust with him. Meaning, you can receive many wonderful blessings even as you wait on God in faith.

Jesus asked the man, "Do you want to get well?" What is it that you want the most in your life right now? What are you waiting to receive?

What role does faith play in waiting for God to move in your life?

What are some steps you can take right now to demonstrate your faith and trust in God while you wait for him to accomplish his will in your life?

A PICTURE OF WAVY FAITH

When you think of the prophets of the Old Testament, you probably picture men and women (hello, Deborah!) of great faith. You might think of individuals who stood against the corrupting tide of culture and cried out, "Thus says the Lord!" You think of prophets as people who got it right on a spiritual level—people who knew what they were doing when it comes to faith.

But then there's Jonah. From the very first moment of Jonah's book, it's clear that he was a different type of prophet. Take a look:

> The word of the LORD came to Jonah son of Amittai: "Go to the great city of Nineveh and preach against it, because its wickedness has come up before me." But Jonah ran away from the LORD and headed for Tarshish. He went down to

Joppa, where he found a ship bound for that port. After paying the fare, he went aboard and sailed for Tarshish to flee from the LORD.

JONAH 1:1–3

Ouch. What basically happened is that God said, "Jonah, go preach my words to your enemies," and Jonah responded by booking a ticket to a place as far away from his enemies as he could find. This was nothing short of disobedience, rebellion, and rejection of God.

In other words, Jonah didn't have it all together spiritually. He was a mess. And—as so often happens—Jonah's rebellion created a mess not just for his own life but also for the lives of the people around him. Here's what happened next:

Then the LORD sent a great wind on the sea, and such a violent storm arose that the ship threatened to break up. All the sailors were afraid and each cried out to his own god. And they threw the cargo into the sea to lighten the ship.

But Jonah had gone below deck, where he lay down and fell into a deep sleep. The captain went to him and said, "How can you sleep? Get up and call on your god! Maybe he will take notice of us so that we will not perish."

Then the sailors said to each other, "Come, let us cast lots to find out who is responsible for this calamity." They cast lots and the lot fell on Jonah. So they asked him, "Tell us, who is responsible for making all this trouble for us? What kind of work do you do? Where do you come from? What is your country? From what people are you?"

He answered, "I am a Hebrew and I worship the LORD, the God of heaven, who made the sea and the dry land."

This terrified them and they asked, "What have you done?" (They knew he was running away from the LORD, because he had already told them so.)

The sea was getting rougher and rougher. So they asked him, "What should we do to you to make the sea calm down for us?"

"Pick me up and throw me into the sea," he replied, "and it will become calm. I know that it is my fault that this great storm has come upon you."

Instead, the men did their best to row back to land. But they could not, for the sea grew even wilder than before. Then they cried out to the LORD, "Please, LORD, do not let us die for taking this man's life. Do not hold us accountable for killing an innocent man, for you, LORD, have done as you pleased." Then they took Jonah and threw him overboard, and the raging sea grew calm. At this the men greatly feared the LORD, and they offered a sacrifice to the LORD and made vows to him.

JONAH 1:4–16

Here's an important truth about wavy faith: it typically presents itself when you find yourself out in the middle of a storm. It's easy to believe you have faith when everything is going your way—when the bank account is full, when your work is meaningful and profitable, when your closest relationships become your deepest sources of joy, and so on. It's easy to claim you have faith when the sun is shining and you've got your toes in the sand.

But *real* faith is revealed when the weather turns rough. And Jonah displayed true faith when the storm hit hardest in his life. Yes, it's true that Jonah was the cause of that storm.

Yes, it's true that he messed up big time by running away from God for his own selfish reasons. Yes, his choice to reject God had put other people at risk.

All of that is true. But when the rubber hit the road, so to speak, Jonah looked the other sailors in the eye and said, "Pick me up and throw me into the sea." Why? As he said, "I know that it is my fault that this great storm has come upon you."

It takes faith to put the good of others ahead of what is good for you. It especially takes faith to lay down your life so that others might live. Make no mistake—Jonah expected to die. He was asking these men to chuck him overboard in the middle of the ocean. There was no Coast Guard or rescue helicopters in that day.

Jonah was telling these men to kill him so that they could survive. That's a picture of wavy faith in action. May we all have what it takes to look out at the clouds and the waves and the lightning and say, "Lord, not my will, but your will be done."

What were the results of Jonah's disobedience in following God's call? What were the results of his eventual obedience?

Read Jonah's prayer in 2:1–9. Where do you see evidence of Jonah's faith in those verses?

Where are you facing something difficult in your life right now—something that presents an opportunity for you to exercise wavy faith?

WALKING IN **Crazy Faith**

Good, bad, or ugly, every circumstance in your life is either God-*used* or God-*sent*. God uses anything and everything to accomplish his ultimate purpose. At times, he may ask you to wait. At times, he may ask you to ask. And at times, he may send you into a storm.

Some people talk about storms being a result of disobedience or distrust in God's plan. But what happens when you run into a storm because you *obeyed* His instructions? When you look at the story of Jesus walking on the stormy sea, you can't escape the fact that it was *Jesus* who instructed the disciples to "get into the boat and go on ahead of him to the other side" (Matthew 14:22). Jesus—being God in the flesh—certainly knew the storm was coming.

So, it was the disciples' obedience to Jesus' command that led to them being in a rocking boat in the middle of a crazy storm. But why? Well, perhaps it was so he could get Peter into the middle of the lake so he could perform one of his greatest miracles through him. Maybe he wanted to test their faith to see if they were ready for where he wanted to take them. Maybe he wanted to use this experience to grow their faith in him.

The same is true in your life. Maybe the storm that God has sent feels terrible but is actually saving your life. Maybe learning to endure and press through this hardship is making you acknowledge your weaknesses and helping you grow stronger in faith and maturity. Maybe it's helping you acknowledge that you have no better choice but to fully rely on God. Maybe where you are is no longer suitable for where God wants to take you.

When you encounter a trying situation, don't be quick to think it was the enemy. Remember, the devil didn't send the disciples into the storm—that was Christ—and he was there with them in the midst of it. So, if you're in the middle of a storm, step back and evaluate: *Did God send this? Did God transport me into this? What does He want me to do or to do in me while I'm here?* If you feel yourself starting to drown, ask yourself, *Have I taken my eyes off Him? Was I listening to someone else's call? Did I send myself into this storm?* If Jesus sent you there, do you really think He's going to allow you to drown? Not at all!

We often want God to fit into our schedule and sign off on our ideas and align with our will—but that's not how faith works. Faith works when we believe for something that God desires for us. We must learn to trust that if He sends us, He will be with us . . . and that even if the situation we are confronting seems completely impossible, He will make a way.[6]

How do you respond to this idea that God will sometimes send you into a storm? When has that happened in your life?

Think of some times in your life when you decided to take matters into your own hands rather than waiting on God. What happened as a result?

Think of some times in your life when you sensed God was calling you to act but you decided to play it safe. What happened as a result?

For Next Session: Write down any insights or questions you want to discuss at the next group meeting. In preparation for the next session, review chapters 6 and 8 in **Crazy Faith**.

SESSION 3
OBSTACLES TO OVERCOME

(LAZY FAITH AND FUGAZI FAITH)
CHAPTER 6   CHAPTER 8

Wake up, sleeper, rise from the dead,
and Christ will shine on you.

EPHESIANS 5:14

WELCOME

The Tour de France is a grueling cycling competition that captures the attention of the world for several weeks each summer. The cyclists who participate are used to overcoming a number of obstacles as they seek to win the prize—inclement weather, bruising mountains, oppressive heat, and even other cyclists. What the athletes are not used to encountering are obstacles caused by spectators. But that is exactly what happened during the first day of racing in 2021.

About twenty-eight miles from the end of that day's circuit, a female spectator suddenly stepped into the road to display a sign for the TV cameras. It read, "Allez Opi Omi," which translates, "Go Grandma and Grandpa," in a combination of French and German. Apparently, this woman was sending a message to her loved ones watching the race back home.

But it was a costly message. The woman's cardboard sign stuck out into the race area and clipped one of the cyclists, who was knocked down. That single incident created a chain reaction that one veteran observer called, "The worst Tour de France crash I've ever seen." Dozens of cyclists went down like dominoes, with competitors clanging against each other and even getting stuck as their handles or pedals locked together.

It took five minutes for crews to separate the cyclists and restart the race. Ten riders had to be treated for injuries, and two had to withdraw from the race. The worst injury was suffered by one cyclist from Spain who broke both of his arms. The woman herself was fined around $1,400 and became the focus of much scorn from the public and media alike.[7]

We're all going to experience obstacles—in cycling, at work, in our relationships, in our personal growth. And yes, we will experience obstacles along our journey toward **crazy**

faith. Sometimes, those obstacles will seem to come out of nowhere, like that cardboard sign. But in this session, we are going to look at two obstacles that we ourselves cause. We can refer to these roadblocks as lazy faith and fugazi faith.

SHARE

Begin your group time by inviting those in the group to share any insights they have from their personal study. Then, to kick things off, discuss one of the following questions:

- How do you typically respond when obstacles get in the way of your plans?

— *or* —

- What obstacles have impacted your spiritual life over the past year?

READ

Invite someone to read aloud the following passage. Listen for fresh insights as you hear the verses being read, and then discuss the questions that follow.

> *Even if I should choose to boast, I would not be a fool, because I would be speaking the truth. But I refrain, so no one will think more of me than is warranted by what I do or say, or because of these surpassingly great revelations. Therefore, in order to keep me from becoming conceited, I was given a thorn in my flesh, a messenger of Satan, to torment me.*

Three times I pleaded with the Lord to take it away from me. But he said to me, "My grace is sufficient for you, for my power is made perfect in weakness." Therefore I will boast all the more gladly about my weaknesses, so that Christ's power may rest on me. That is why, for Christ's sake, I delight in weaknesses, in insults, in hardships, in persecutions, in difficulties. For when I am weak, then I am strong.

2 CORINTHIANS 12:6–10

What kind of obstacle does Paul say that he was confronting in his ministry?

What does it look like to "delight in weaknesses" as a follower of Christ?

WATCH

Watch the video segment for session three. (Play the DVD or see the instructions on the inside front cover on how to access the sessions through streaming.) As you and your group watch, use the following outline to record any thoughts or concepts that stand out to you.

We all have a side of ourselves that finds it easier to fake it than be real. This is why it is important to stay vigilant in our quest for 𝕮𝖗𝖆𝖟𝖞 𝕱𝖆𝖎𝖙𝖍. The type of faith God rewards is both active and authentic.

Lazy faith is innate in all of us. There's a part of us that procrastinates and likes to think we have another moment and another time to do something. But the reality is that many times that time never comes.

It's important to have a faith that is active, alive, and that other people can see, because you may be the only Bible some people read. *Your life* is what people are going to see.

The four men who brought their paralyzed friend to Jesus could have quit when they saw the crowds. But they persevered and were committed to finding a different way to get their friend in front of Christ.

We need to stay away from fugazi faith. Fugazi means fake, counterfeit, and not real. This is a kind of faith that doesn't really believe but acts like it does.

Mary and Martha demonstrated authentic faith after the death of their brother. They believed in Jesus so much that even in the midst of their devastation, they were able to communicate how disappointed they were, but also that they believed Jesus could still move in the situation.

God's glory showed up at Lazarus's tomb. Likewise, when you have authentic faith, you can look at something that should be a graveyard and it can become a garden. It can become a place of life.

It's time for us to believe in authentic, strong, 𝕮𝖗𝖆𝖟𝖞 𝕱𝖆𝖎𝖙𝖍. It is time for us to be done with lazy faith and fugazi faith. God will do everything we *can't* do . . . but nothing that we *can*.

DISCUSS

As you consider what you just watched, use the following questions to discuss these ideas, their basis in Scripture, and their application in your life with your group members.

1. What are the dangers of procrastination when it comes to your faith?

2. How would you describe lazy faith? How is it different from active faith?

3. Read Mark 2:1–12. What can you learn about faith by comparing the actions of the four friends of the paralyzed man against the words of the teachers of the law?

4. How would you describe fugazi faith? How is it different from authentic faith?

5. Read John 11:17–44. What are some ways that this story demonstrates that Mary and Martha had not only waiting faith but also authentic faith?

6. What are steps you can take to remove lazy faith and fugazi faith from your life?

RESPOND

Briefly review the outline for the video teaching and any notes you took. Write down your responses to these two questions: (1) Where am I currently struggling with lazy faith? (2) What are some symptoms that would reveal fugazi faith in my life?

PRAY

As you close your time together, affirm the truth that God will accomplish everything that you *can't* do—but nothing that you *can*. Ask him to help you remove any traces of lazy faith and fugazi faith in your life so you can live in active, genuine, **Crazy Faith**. Use the space below to record any specific prayer requests or praises that you have for the group.

Name	Request/Praise

PERSONAL STUDY

Reflect on the material you covered during the group time by engaging in any or all of the following between-session activities. Be sure to read the reflection questions and make a few notes in your guide about the experience. At the start of your next group session, you will have a few minutes to share any insights that you learned.

A PICTURE OF LAZY FAITH

In the disciples' defense, it had been a long day. It had all begun with a trip down the Mount of Olives into Jerusalem for the first day of the annual Passover festival. Now, Passover was a major moment on the Jewish calendar, which means that tens of thousands of pilgrims had descended on Jerusalem to celebrate. There were huge crowds in the city, and many of the people in those crowds pressed Jesus (and the disciples) wherever he went.

The regular folk weren't the only ones seeking out Jesus. The Pharisees and the teachers of the law had stepped up their campaign to discredit him while he was in Jerusalem. They pestered him with questions and hypothetical situations. They pushed him to say something that they considered heretical so they could have him prosecuted under their law.

Finally, after a day spent pushing through crowds and fending off Pharisees, the disciples and Jesus finally had a chance to rest and enjoy a Passover meal. But this did not prove to be an easy meal. Instead, Jesus used this "Last Supper" as a teaching and preparation—though the disciples had no idea what they were experiencing or what was to come.

After all that—with their bellies and brains fit to burst—Jesus led the disciples back up the Mount of Olives and into a garden. Matthew details what happened next:

> Then Jesus went with his disciples to a place called Gethsemane, and he said to them, "Sit here while I go over there and pray." He took Peter and the two sons of Zebedee along with him, and he began to be sorrowful and troubled. Then he said to them, "My soul is overwhelmed with sorrow to the point of death. Stay here and keep watch with me."
>
> Going a little farther, he fell with his face to the ground and prayed, "My Father, if it is possible, may this cup be taken from me. Yet not as I will, but as you will."
>
> Then he returned to his disciples and found them sleeping. "Couldn't you men keep watch with me for one hour?" he asked Peter. "Watch and pray so that you will not fall into temptation. The spirit is willing, but the flesh is weak."
>
> He went away a second time and prayed, "My Father, if it is not possible for this cup to be taken away unless I drink it, may your will be done."

When he came back, he again found them sleeping, because their eyes were heavy. So he left them and went away once more and prayed the third time, saying the same thing.

Then he returned to the disciples and said to them, "Are you still sleeping and resting? Look, the hour has come, and the Son of Man is delivered into the hands of sinners. Rise! Let us go! Here comes my betrayer!"

MATTHEW 26:36–46

Yes, it had been a long day. But still, that didn't excuse Peter, James, and John for what happened in Gethsemane that night. Jesus, their Savior, Lord, Master, and Rabbi had asked for help. "My soul is overwhelmed with sorrow to the point of death," he had told them. "Stay here and keep watch with me." But they didn't. They fell asleep. They let Jesus down.

Sadly, we all do the same thing. Sure, we see that opportunity to step up and serve. We know we have the skills to do it. We even feel the Holy Spirit nudging us to act. But then we consider how much time and effort it will take on our part. We quickly rationalize there are others "more qualified" to do it. In the end, we ignore the request from our Lord.

Here's the reality. *Anytime* we choose our own comfort over the work God has called us to do, we are drifting into lazy faith. And there will be consequences.

What are some of the ways that you sense God is asking you to serve him and to serve others in this season of your life?

What personal desires or comforts have gotten in the way of you stepping up to serve?

How do you handle this tension between what you want to do and what God wants you to do?

A PICTURE OF FUGAZI FAITH

Religion and money have always been a bad combination when it comes to genuine spirituality. But religion and money have proven to be a fantastic combination when it comes to creating wealth and exercising control over others. For those reasons, the combination of religion and money is a major source of the fugazi faith we often experience in our culture.

But it's not just in our culture. At the beginning of the church, we see that combination not only present but also threatening to do damage. Take a look at this story from Acts:

> *Now for some time a man named Simon had practiced sorcery in the city and amazed all the people of Samaria.*

He boasted that he was someone great, and all the people, both high and low, gave him their attention and exclaimed, "This man is rightly called the Great Power of God." They followed him because he had amazed them for a long time with his sorcery. But when they believed Philip as he proclaimed the good news of the kingdom of God and the name of Jesus Christ, they were baptized, both men and women. Simon himself believed and was baptized. And he followed Philip everywhere, astonished by the great signs and miracles he saw.

When the apostles in Jerusalem heard that Samaria had accepted the word of God, they sent Peter and John to Samaria. When they arrived, they prayed for the new believers there that they might receive the Holy Spirit, because the Holy Spirit had not yet come on any of them; they had simply been baptized in the name of the Lord Jesus. Then Peter and John placed their hands on them, and they received the Holy Spirit.

When Simon saw that the Spirit was given at the laying on of the apostles' hands, he offered them money and said, "Give me also this ability so that everyone on whom I lay my hands may receive the Holy Spirit."

Peter answered: "May your money perish with you, because you thought you could buy the gift of God with money! You have no part or share in this ministry, because your heart is not right before God. Repent of this wickedness and pray to the Lord in the hope that he may forgive you for having such a thought in your heart. For I see that you are full of bitterness and captive to sin."

Then Simon answered, "Pray to the Lord for me so that nothing you have said may happen to me."

After they had further proclaimed the word of the Lord
and testified about Jesus, Peter and John returned to Jerusa-
lem, preaching the gospel in many Samaritan villages.

ACTS 8:9–25

Simon the Sorcerer is a picture of fugazi faith. He wasn't interested in God. He wasn't interested in serving others. He wasn't interested in spiritual growth, spiritual disciplines, or spiritual fruit. He was only interested in himself and his own personal gain, and he saw the positive elements demonstrated by the early Christians as means to an end for his own glory.

The spirit of Simon the Sorcerer is still alive today. There are still those who use the trappings of Christianity to advance themselves and their own goals. Such people cause great harm both in our culture and in the church. Thankfully, Jesus gave us a handy tool for identifying such people in our midst. Here is what he said to his followers:

"Watch out for false prophets. They come to you in sheep's
clothing, but inwardly they are ferocious wolves. By their fruit
you will recognize them. Do people pick grapes from thorn-
bushes, or figs from thistles? Likewise, every good tree bears
good fruit, but a bad tree bears bad fruit. A good tree cannot
bear bad fruit, and a bad tree cannot bear good fruit. Every
tree that does not bear good fruit is cut down and thrown into
the fire. Thus, by their fruit you will recognize them.

MATTHEW 7:15–20

You can't produce spiritual fruit with fugazi faith. So, when you find yourself in a community that is producing true "good fruit" for the kingdom of God, dive right in! Jump in with both feet and join that community in demonstrating authentic faith.

How do you see the combination of religion and money causing harm in today's culture?

Read Acts 8:26–40. How does Philip serve as a picture of authentic faith?

What "good fruit" is being produced in your life that indicates you have an authentic faith?

WALKING IN Crazy Faith

When you read the story in Luke 5:17–26 of the four guys who dug a hole in the roof so they could lower their paralyzed friend down to Jesus, you'll notice that the Bible never reveals their names. Luke only refers to them as "some men" (verse 18). They have no description or titles. There is no mention of their race, class, or socioeconomic status. We don't know if they were celebrities or bums. We don't hear another word about them after the events of that day.

If some of us were in this story, we would be posing on the rooftop and shouting out, "Hey, y'all are putting this in the Bible, right? Make sure you spell my name right—and tag me on the 'gram!" Many of us wouldn't be okay with no one knowing our name. We would be boasting all over town about how we played a part in getting our buddy healed . . . even though Jesus was the one who did all the heavy lifting. We would want credit for every ounce of effort.

But it doesn't seem as if these "some men" were concerned about getting their pictures in the local paper, or getting tagged, or whatever. They were far more focused on helping their friend experience lasting transformation and playing a part in his future testimony. These men were not only willing to *do* the work but also were to do the work without a *credit*.

These "some men" volunteered to be ministers and attend to their paralyzed friend's needs. As a matter of fact, we keep referring to them as "friends," but the Bible doesn't actually say they were part of the paralyzed man's crew. There is no specific indication that relationship or obligation was influencing them to act on their faith that day. All we know is that they did what needed to be done so that a hurting man could see Jesus and receive his healing.

Active faith gets credit in eternity. Some of the things that God is calling you to do may not be seen by others on this side of heaven. The work you do behind the scenes may not be publicly recognized. As Paul says, "Whatever you do, work at it with all your heart, as working for the Lord, not for human masters, since you know that you will receive an inheritance from the Lord as a reward. It is the Lord Christ you are serving" (Colossians 3:23–24).

Be content to serve God, just like these "some men" in Luke's story. We can all take a lesson from these nameless heroes of crazy faith.[8]

What types of actions or attitudes does our culture celebrate and lift up today?

Who are examples of people in your life who consistently serve God without seeking credit?

It takes faith to serve God without seeking credit. Where do you have an opportunity to demonstrate that kind of faith in this season of your life?

For Next Session: Write down any insights or questions you want to discuss at the next group meeting. In preparation for the next session, review chapters 7 and 9 in **Crazy Faith**.

SESSION 4
MOVING TO THE NEXT LEVEL
(TRADING FAITH AND STATING FAITH)
CHAPTER 7
CHAPTER 9

Like newborn babies, crave pure spiritual milk,
so that by it you may grow up in your salvation.

1 PETER 2:2

WELCOME

Here's a question for you. How many students do you think there currently are in the United States? We're talking about all grades—kindergarten through the senior year of high school. And we're talking all types of schools—public, private, charter, home schools, and so on. How many kids do you think attend a school of some kind on a typical day in the United States?

The answer is just over fifty million. That's the estimate based on the best federal data available for the 2022 school year.[9] That's a lot of students! Just try to get your mind around fifty million kids out on the roads every weekday morning in buses or cars, getting themselves mentally ready for another day of school. Think about fifty million backpacks full of books and notebooks and pencils and who knows what else. Or fifty million pens and pencils scribbling out answers to fifty million homework assignments.

What is the goal for each of those fifty million kids? To get to the next level. These students want to keep moving forward in their education so they can grow and develop into the women and men they were created to be. (Yeah, it's true that's not the specific goal of *every* student—but let's hope it's the overall goal of the school system.)

Funny enough, you are working toward the same goal. Not graduation necessarily, but moving to the next level—financially, relationally, vocationally, and yes, spiritually in your journey toward 𝖈𝖗𝖆𝖟𝖞 𝖋𝖆𝖎𝖙𝖍. So far in that journey, we've explored several basic elements of faith, including baby faith, maybe faith, waiting faith, and wavy faith. We've also highlighted two types of faith that we need to avoid: lazy faith and fugazi faith.

In this session, it's time to take things to the next level by digging into what we might call trading faith and stating faith. Let's jump in and get started!

SHARE

Begin your group time by inviting those in the group to share any insights they have from their personal study. Then, to kick things off, discuss one of the following questions:

- What are some of the major goals you have achieved in your life?

— *or* —

- What does the "next level" look like for you when it comes to your faith?

READ

Invite someone to read aloud the following passage. Listen for fresh insights as you hear the verses being read, and then discuss the questions that follow.

His divine power has given us everything we need for a godly life through our knowledge of him who called us by his own glory and goodness. Through these he has given us his very great and precious promises, so that through them you may participate in the divine nature, having escaped the corruption in the world caused by evil desires.

For this very reason, make every effort to add to your faith goodness; and to goodness, knowledge; and to knowledge, self-control; and to self-control, perseverance; and to perseverance, godliness; and to godliness, mutual affection; and to mutual affection, love. For if you possess these qualities in increasing measure, they will keep you from being ineffective and unproductive in your knowledge of our Lord Jesus Christ. But whoever does not have them is nearsighted and blind, forgetting that they have been cleansed from their past sins.

2 PETER 1:3–9

Do you feel like you have "everything" you need to lead a godly life? Why or why not?

Peter describes a progression of godly attributes that you can add to your life when you start with faith. Which of those attributes feels most needed in today's culture?

WATCH

Watch the video segment for session four. (Play the DVD or see the instructions on the inside front cover on how to access the sessions through streaming.) As you and your group watch, use the following outline to record any thoughts or concepts that stand out to you.

God is looking for those who are willing to step out, step up, and speak out as he directs. He can take your paperclip-sized faith and grow it into faith the size of a house and beyond.

There comes a moment in your journey where you have to trade in the faith that got you to this point for a faith that will get you to the next level. You have to start to believe for yourself.

The faith victories you have experienced in the past do not guarantee that you will experience faith victories in the future. At times, you will need to trade in your faith so you can receive something better.

Jesus saw the faith of the men who had lowered the paralyzed man down through the roof and immediately forgave him of his sins. He then gave the man three instructions to follow:

Stand up: have the faith to try something that seems impossible

Pick up your mat: trade in your faith but not your testimony

Go home: show the people in your world what God has done

One of the clear signs that your faith is moving to the next level is when you start to change what you say. You start to speak in victory and state your faith, knowing the God of the universe is backing you.

The words you speak can actually change the world you are living in right now. But the truth of the matter is that many of us are too scared to say what we are really believing God to do in our lives.

Bartimaeus called to Jesus out of his impossible situation because he knew there was a possibility that his life could be transformed. When Jesus heard him, he asked, "What do you want?" He gave the blind man an opportunity to *state* in faith what he wanted God to accomplish in and through his life.

Thinking about faith is not enough. You have to speak the language of faith. So don't just think it or wish it—confidently *state* your faith.

DISCUSS

As you consider what you just watched, use the following questions to discuss these ideas, their basis in Scripture, and their application in your life with your group members.

1. What would you say has gotten you to this point in your spiritual journey? What disciplines or routines or practices have been important for you?

2. How would you describe what it means to exercise trading faith?

3. Read Luke 5:17–26. What is something "remarkable" that you would like to see take place in your life or in the lives of those you care about?

4. How would you describe what it means to exercise stating faith?

5. What do you feel are some of the bigger obstacles that hinder followers of Christ from talking about God or sharing what he values with the people in the world?

6. Read Mark 10:46–52. What are ways you can state what you want God to do for you?

RESPOND

Briefly review the outline for the video teaching and any notes you took. Write down your responses to these two questions: (1) What do I need to "trade in" when it comes to my faith so that God can move me to the next level? (2) What are some situations in my life right now where I need to exercise stating faith and proclaim God's victories?

PRAY

As you close your time together, take a few moments to reflect on Jesus' question to Bartimaeus: "What do you want me to do for you?" Express your answer to the group if you feel comfortable doing so. Also consider expressing your willingness to let go of what brought you to this point in your faith so you can experience the next level of what God desires for you. Use the space below to record any prayer requests or praises you have for the group.

Name   **Request/Praise**

PERSONAL STUDY

Reflect on the material you covered during the group time by engaging in any or all of the following between-session activities. Be sure to read the reflection questions and make a few notes in your guide about the experience. At the start of your next group session, you will have a few minutes to share any insights that you learned.

A PICTURE OF TRADING FAITH

Here's a fun fact: there are thirty-four people who have books of the Bible named after them—people such as Joshua, Ruth, Samuel, Esther, Matthew, John, Luke, and James. Talk about an exclusive club!

One of those people is a young man named Timothy. (Actually, he has two books named after him—1 and 2 Timothy.) We don't know a lot about Timothy as a person, but we do know that he was mentored in the faith by the apostle Paul, served alongside Paul in several churches, and eventually became a key leader of the early church in his own right. Here is what Paul said to him at the beginning of the second epistle that bears Timothy's name:

> *I thank God, whom I serve, as my ancestors did, with a clear conscience, as night and day I constantly remember you in my prayers. Recalling your tears, I long to see you, so that I may be filled with joy. I am reminded of your sincere faith, which first lived in your grandmother Lois and in your mother Eunice and, I am persuaded, now lives in you also.*
>
> 2 TIMOTHY 1:3–5

What's interesting about this passage is that we learn Timothy was one of the first people who experienced the privilege of growing up in a Christian home. His grandma was a follower of Jesus, and so was his mom. Those faithful women must have been vocal about their testimony, because their faith inspired Timothy to trust in Jesus as well. As we read in the book of Acts, this faith of Timothy made him stand out when Paul encountered him in Lystra:

> *Paul came to Derbe and then to Lystra, where a disciple named Timothy lived, whose mother was Jewish and a believer but whose father was a Greek. The believers at Lystra and Iconium spoke well of him. Paul wanted to take him along on the journey, so he circumcised him because of the Jews who lived in that area, for they all knew that his father was a Greek. As they traveled from town to town, they delivered the decisions reached by the apostles and elders in Jerusalem for the people to obey. So the churches were strengthened in the faith and grew daily in numbers.*
>
> ACTS 16:1–5

Notice what happened to Timothy in that moment. He faced a choice. On the one hand, he could accept Paul's offer and join him on his missionary journeys. There was excitement in that offer—a future filled with new places to go, new things to learn, new people to serve, and new dangers to face. On the other hand, Timothy could continue living the life he had always known—stay with Mom and Grandma and keep faithfully doing what he had always been doing. There was comfort in that life. Familiarity and safety.

Please note that Timothy could *not* have both options. He had to choose one or the other. Specifically, in order to join Paul and reach the next level of his faith, Timothy had to trade in all the familiar elements of his faith that had gotten him to that point in his life. He had to let it all go so that he could grab something new . . . something better.

The same is true for you and me.

Read Acts 16:16–40. What risks was Timothy taking by joining Paul and his team of evangelists?

What risks was Timothy taking if he rejected Paul's offer and chose to stay at home?

What risks do you sense God is calling you to take when it comes to trading in your old life and your old comforts and habits for something brand new?

A PICTURE OF STATING FAITH

The book of Numbers describes a pretty rough moment in the life of Moses. Typically, we think of Moses being a great leader (which he was) or even as being as close to perfect as a person can get (which he definitely was not). But this was a bad day for the leader of God's chosen people—and not just for Moses but also for the entire Israelite community.

You see, Moses was being confronted by 250 leaders of the Israelite community. These men were elders in the community—men who were respected, wealthy, and carried a lot of clout. The group of rebels was led by a man named Korah, a Levite, which meant that he had a measure of spiritual authority. He and his 250 buddies were saying to Moses, "You have gone too far! The whole community is holy, every one of them, and the LORD is with them. Why then do you set yourselves above the LORD's assembly?" (Numbers 16:3).

In other words, what Korah and the rebels were saying was, "Moses, why are you setting yourself up as the only one who knows what God wants for his people? Why do you act like you're better than the rest of us? It's time for someone else to be in charge." After a series of escalating confrontations, the whole assembly of Israel ended up standing before God to see what he would say. Moses and Aaron were on one side, while Korah, Dathan, Abiram, and their 250 rebels were on the other. The community watched and waited.

Here's what happened next:

Moses got up and went to Dathan and Abiram, and the elders of Israel followed him. He warned the assembly, "Move back from the tents of these wicked men! Do not touch anything belonging to them, or you will be swept away because of all their sins." So they moved away from the tents of Korah, Dathan and Abiram. Dathan and Abiram had come out and were standing with their wives, children and little ones at the entrances to their tents.

Then Moses said, "This is how you will know that the LORD has sent me to do all these things and that it was not my idea: If these men die a natural death and suffer the fate of all mankind, then the LORD has not sent me. But if the LORD brings about something totally new, and the earth opens its mouth and swallows them, with everything that belongs to them, and they go down alive into the realm of the dead, then you will know that these men have treated the LORD with contempt."

As soon as he finished saying all this, the ground under them split apart and the earth opened its mouth and swallowed them and their households, and all those associated with Korah, together with their possessions. They went down alive into the realm of the dead, with everything they owned; the earth closed over them, and they perished and were gone from the community. At their cries, all the Israelites around them fled, shouting, "The earth is going to swallow us too!"

And fire came out from the LORD and consumed the 250 men who were offering the incense.

NUMBERS 16:25–35

Try to picture Moses in that moment. He was standing in front of the entire community and basically commanded the ground to open up and swallow those who were leading Israel astray. Notice that Moses didn't put a lot of flowery words around his prayer. He didn't say, "God *might* you be able to do this?" or, "God, if it's your will, could you possibly consider doing that?" No, he stated out loud, with his words, what he wanted God to do.

This is an example of *stating faith*. Moses was so confident in his position with God that he stated what needed to happen—in front of everybody—and trusted God to follow through. Now, this is not to say that you should pray for your enemies to be swallowed up by a giant sinkhole. That is not the point of this story. Rather, the point is that there is tremendous power inherent in the act of verbally stating what you need from God—especially when you speak those needs in front of others. That is what it means to demonstrate stating faith.

When have you seen someone demonstrate stating faith in a meaningful way? What happened as a result of that person stating his or her faith?

Read Philippians 4:6–7. How do those verses add to your understanding of stating faith?

Think about a situation you are facing right now where you need God to intervene. How could you state what you want God to do like Moses did in this story?

WALKING IN Crazy Faith

God is a miracle worker, and he dwells inside humans who are always in need of miracles. All of us face impossible situations that need God's intervention. But not all of us experience the fullness of God's omnipotent power working on our behalf. Many times, it's because we lack faith to believe that he can and will do something amazing for us, in us, or through us.

But Crazy Faith states you can be the *exception*. What happened in another situation does not determine what happens in this one. Your perception of previous patterns is not an accurate indicator of future possibilities. There's always an exception. Why can't it be you?

This is not a declaration of superiority but of distinction. You are *no better* than anyone else, but you *are different from* everyone else. This means you can't look at anyone else's life and decide what God wants to do with *you*. This also means that you don't have to be limited by them, governed by them, imprisoned by them, or defined by them. While you may go through the same things that others have gone through, it doesn't automatically mean that you will come out the same way they did. You are living your own story.

You *can* be the exception. But remember that God makes exceptions only in response to faith. People often cry out, "Lord, why me?" when they find themselves in the middle of impossible situations. But you can change your mindset and say, "Lord, why not me?"

Lord, if you're going to allow someone to be the last person accepted into that university . . . why not me? Lord, if You're going to heal someone . . . why not me? Lord, if you're going to restore someone from depression . . . why not my friend? Lord, if you're going to turn someone's heart . . . why not my father's? Lord, if you're going to bring reconciliation to someone, why not my family? My city? My business? My relationships? Why not me?

The Bible is filled with numerous examples of people who became the exception to the rule of what would normally be considered possible. Sarah was in her nineties when she gave birth to a son. The Israelites escaped the Egyptian army by crossing through the Red Sea on dry land. Joshua secured the people's first victory in the promised land by marching around the city of Jericho and then witnessing its walls fall down. Shadrach, Meshach, and Abednego went into a fiery furnace and came out burn free. Daniel went into a lions' den and came out the next day to tell the tale. Jesus fed five thousand people with two fish and five loaves of bread.

All these examples are just the tip of the iceberg. Our omnipotent God is still in the business of making exceptions. And *you* can certainly be one of them.[10]

How easy or difficult is it for you to believe that God can make an exception in your life? What would it take for you to truly believe that all things are possible for him?

Where are you currently making assumptions about what will happen in your life based on what has happened to others?

Where do you have an opportunity right now to ask God to make you an *exception*?

For Next Session: Write down any insights or questions you want to discuss at the next group meeting. In preparation for the next session, review chapters 10–11 in 𝕮𝖗𝖆𝖟𝖞 𝕱𝖆𝖎𝖙𝖍.

SESSION 5

FINISHING STRONG

(FADING FAITH AND SAVING FAITH)
CHAPTER 10   CHAPTER 11

If you declare with your mouth, "Jesus is Lord,"
and believe in your heart that God raised him from
the dead, you will be saved.

ROMANS 10:9

WELCOME

What does it take to speak out against a policy of racial segregation and inequality that has been sanctioned by the government and in existence for decades? Well, it certainly takes courage to stand up for your beliefs in the face of oppression. It takes confidence in knowing that what you are doing is right. And it takes an ability to respond to those who doubt your sanity and question why you would put your life at stake for the cause.

Bishop Desmond Tutu could never have imagined that his actions against the system of apartheid in South Africa would aid in its demise during his lifetime. The policy, first introduced into law in 1950, dictated where South Africans—solely on the basis of their race—could live and work, the type of education they could receive, and whether they could vote. Non-whites were stripped of their rights, forced to live in regions away from the white population, and discriminated against at every level of society.

The government of South Africa held the power to suppress all criticism against apartheid. Regardless, Desmond Tutu, and others like him, chose to use their platform to speak out against the system and raise international awareness as to what was actually happening in the country. His efforts led to a public outcry across the world and countries such as the United States and the United Kingdom imposing economic sanctions against South Africa in 1985. Ultimately, the government was forced to start repealing the unjust laws in early 1990.

Bishop Desmond Tutu retired from his public duties in 2010 but remained committed to securing equal rights for blacks until his death in 2021. What's interesting is that toward the end of his life, he admitted to often being angry with God at the lack of progress he was seeing. In one interview, he stated, "I've remonstrated with God quite frequently and said, 'What are you up to? Why are you letting these oppressors get away with this injustice?'"[11]

In our journey toward 𝕮𝖗𝖆𝖟𝖞 𝕱𝖆𝖎𝖙𝖍, we will encounter bumps along the way that may cause us to question what God is doing. We will experience times when it seems that our faith is fading. But it is in those moments that we will see God at work in our lives . . . and our faith will be strengthened as we focus on him and the hope that he has provided through our salvation.

SHARE

Begin your group time by inviting those in the group to share any insights they have from their personal study. Then, to kick things off, discuss one of the following questions:

- When are times that your faith seemed to fade? What happened in your life that re-energized your faith?

— *or* —

- What are some of the lessons you have learned through times of failure?

READ

Invite someone to read aloud the following passage. Listen for fresh insights as you hear the verses being read, and then discuss the questions that follow.

In the presence of God and of Christ Jesus, who will judge the living and the dead, and in view of his appearing and his kingdom, I give you this charge: Preach the word; be prepared in season and out of season; correct, rebuke and encourage— with great patience and careful instruction. For the time will come when people will not put up with sound doctrine. Instead, to suit their own desires, they will gather around them a great number of teachers to say what their itching ears want to hear. They will turn their ears away from the truth and turn aside to myths. But you, keep your head in all situations, endure hardship, do the work of an evangelist, discharge all the duties of your ministry.

For I am already being poured out like a drink offering, and the time for my departure is near. I have fought the good fight, I have finished the race, I have kept the faith. Now there is in store for me the crown of righteousness, which the Lord, the righteous Judge, will award to me on that day—and not only to me, but also to all who have longed for his appearing.

2 TIMOTHY 4:1–8

Which of Paul's warnings from this passage resonates most deeply with you right now? Why?

What does it look like for you to "finish the race" in this season of your faith journey?

WATCH

Watch the video segment for session five. (Play the DVD or see the instructions on the inside front cover on how to access the sessions through streaming.) As you and your group watch, use the following outline to record any thoughts or concepts that stand out to you.

Those times when it feels like your faith is fading isn't an indication something is wrong with you or the vision that God has placed in your heart. Instead, it is an indication you need to reconnect with the author and the finisher of your faith. When you do, you will see crazy things start to happen in your life.

We will experience amazing things on the journey toward **Crazy Faith**. But we will also work through some dark days and struggles that may shake us to the core. Those can lead to fading faith.

It's hard to maintain faith at times, especially when we don't see progress. We don't live on mountaintops all the time. Valleys are a part of the landscape for believers as well. The truth of the matter is that fading faith may be a part of your journey, but it does not have to end there.

The disciple Thomas gets a bad rap because he had a moment of doubt when he heard the reports that Jesus was raised from the dead. But even though he had fading faith, the other disciples didn't throw him out. They let him stay with them, even in his doubts . . . and God showed up again.

The good news is that you hope through Jesus Christ. You have access to saving faith. Jesus is the way, the truth, and the life, no matter how dark your situation may be right now.

The idea of Mary being pregnant while still being a virgin was crazy. It was a *crazy word* that both Mary and Joseph had to wrestle with, and it caused some *crazy worry* in their lives.

Mary and Joseph took their worry to God in prayer, and he enabled them to move forward in a *crazy walk* toward Bethlehem. This was part of God's *crazy way* of providing salvation for all people.

Whatever God does for your business, your family, or your future, it's so that people can see his goodness and be drawn to him. He wants everybody to find saving faith. When God blesses you, your family, your business, and your friends, everyone will see that he is good and will be drawn to him.

DISCUSS

As you consider what you just watched, use the following questions to discuss these ideas, their basis in Scripture, and their application in your life with your group members.

1. What are some elements of life that are testing or trying your faith right now?

2. How would you summarize what it means to experience times of fading faith?

3. Read John 20:19–29. What are the main reasons or sources of evidence that help you "believe" in Jesus' death and resurrection?

4. How would you describe what it means to have saving faith in Christ?

5. Read Matthew 1:18–25. What are some ways that Joseph demonstrated his faith?

6. What is the next step you want to take on your journey toward 𝕮𝖗𝖆𝖟𝖞 𝕱𝖆𝖎𝖙𝖍?

RESPOND

Briefly review the outline for the video teaching and any notes you took. Take a few moments to consider what truths about the gospel you could share with someone to help him or her experience God's saving faith. Write down those truths in the space below.

PRAY

As you close this study, pray as a group for those friends, family members, coworkers, and others who need to experience saving faith. Pray for each person specifically by name. Use the space below to record any final prayer requests or praises you have for the group.

Name | **Request/Praise**

_____ | _____

_____ | _____

_____ | _____

_____ | _____

_____ | _____

_____ | _____

_____ | _____

_____ | _____

_____ | _____

_____ | _____

_____ | _____

_____ | _____

PERSONAL STUDY

Reflect on the material you covered during your final group time by engaging in any or all of the following activities. Be sure to read the reflection questions and make a few notes in your guide about the experience. Consider sharing these insights with your group members in the days and weeks following the conclusion of this study.

A PICTURE OF FADING FAITH

It was a strange time for the disciple Peter. On one hand, his Master was alive! Jesus had defeated death and the grave. He had proven his resurrection by revealing himself to the disciples on several occasions—even allowing Thomas to place his hand on his wounds.

Peter, as you might recall, had denied even knowing Jesus on the night that he was arrested. And not just once . . . but *three* times. Standing there in the courtyard, he had been close enough to Jesus to see him lift his head and look directly at him. Peter knew that Jesus knew that he had betrayed him. He had wept bitterly as a result of his shame.

But now Jesus was *alive*. What would happen next? Would Jesus chide him for his actions? Could their relationship ever be restored? It was a tense season.

One day, in the midst of all that tension, Peter decided that he'd had enough. "I'm going out to fish," he announced. That's important. Why? Because Peter had been a fisherman before Jesus had called him to "fish for people." In the midst of his frustration and uncertainty after the resurrection, Peter was taking a step away from 𝖈𝖗𝖆𝖟𝖞 𝖋𝖆𝖎𝖙𝖍 and toward his *old way* of life.

He was likely experiencing a season of fading faith. Read what happens next:

> *Afterward Jesus appeared again to his disciples, by the Sea of Galilee. It happened this way: Simon Peter, Thomas (also known as Didymus), Nathanael from Cana in Galilee, the sons of Zebedee, and two other disciples were together. "I'm going out to fish," Simon Peter told them, and they said, "We'll go with you." So they went out and got into the boat, but that night they caught nothing.*
>
> *Early in the morning, Jesus stood on the shore, but the disciples did not realize that it was Jesus.*
>
> *He called out to them, "Friends, haven't you any fish?"*
>
> *"No," they answered.*
>
> *He said, "Throw your net on the right side of the boat and you will find some." When they did, they were unable to haul the net in because of the large number of fish.*
>
> *Then the disciple whom Jesus loved said to Peter, "It is the Lord!" As soon as Simon Peter heard him say, "It is the*

Lord," he wrapped his outer garment around him (for he had taken it off) and jumped into the water. The other disciples followed in the boat, towing the net full of fish, for they were not far from shore, about a hundred yards. When they landed, they saw a fire of burning coals there with fish on it, and some bread.

JOHN 21:1-9

You have to love Jesus' timing. Just as Peter and the other disciples were starting to drift backward into their old ways of life, he appears on the scene. He calls them back to the journey of crazy faith with yet another proof of His power . . . *and they respond.* In Peter's case, he literally dove headfirst into the new life that Jesus was calling him to lead.

May we do the same!

What are some actions, attitudes, or practices that represent your old way of life?

The source of Peter's fading faith was likely his denial of Jesus on the night that he was arrested. Read John 21:15–19. How did Jesus heal Peter of that denial?

When have you been tempted to drift backward to your old way of life? What steps can you take today to dive back into God's plan?

A PICTURE OF SAVING FAITH

It probably doesn't surprise you that there are many stories in the Bible about people encountering God for the first time. After all, it's the Bible! But one salvation story that stands out occurs in Acts 8. It is a story that shows just how powerful saving faith can be when God is at work in someone's life. Take a look at the story from the book of Acts:

> Now an angel of the Lord said to Philip, "Go south to the road—the desert road—that goes down from Jerusalem to Gaza." So he started out, and on his way he met an Ethiopian eunuch, an important official in charge of all the treasury of the Kandake (which means "queen of the Ethiopians"). This man had gone to Jerusalem to worship, and on his way home was sitting in his chariot reading the Book of Isaiah the prophet. The Spirit told Philip, "Go to that chariot and stay near it."
>
> Then Philip ran up to the chariot and heard the man reading Isaiah the prophet. "Do you understand what you are reading?" Philip asked.
>
> "How can I," he said, "unless someone explains it to me?" So he invited Philip to come up and sit with him.

This is the passage of Scripture the eunuch was reading:

"He was led like a sheep to the slaughter,
and as a lamb before its shearer is silent,
so he did not open his mouth.
In his humiliation he was deprived of justice.
Who can speak of his descendants?
For his life was taken from the earth."

The eunuch asked Philip, "Tell me, please, who is the prophet talking about, himself or someone else?" Then Philip began with that very passage of Scripture and told him the good news about Jesus.

As they traveled along the road, they came to some water and the eunuch said, "Look, here is water. What can stand in the way of my being baptized?" And he gave orders to stop the chariot. Then both Philip and the eunuch went down into the water and Philip baptized him.

ACTS 8:26–38

Don't miss the fact that this was a foreigner from Ethiopia who had traveled all the way to Jerusalem to worship God. Meaning, God had already been at work in his life. Also notice that this man wasn't just a random wanderer. He was an important official. He served the "Kandake," which was likely a title (like Pharaoh) for the leader of his nation.

So, this man was chilling in his chariot reading God's Word . . . and he was confused. In that same moment, the Holy Spirit reached out to Philip the apostle and said, essentially, "I got some work for you to do. Get going." And Philip obeyed.

Look at how natural the conversation flowed between Philip and the Ethiopian. Philip wasn't worried about following any formula or saying the right things to "convince" this man about the truth of the gospel. He just started out by meeting the Ethiopian exactly where he was. "Do you understand what you are reading?" he said. A simple question, but also profound.

We often think of evangelism as talking people into salvation—as if everything depends on our words, skill, and intelligence. But evangelism is simply being willing to get caught up in what God is already doing. This means looking for places where God is working—looking for people to whom God is speaking—and then making yourself available. "How can I help?"

That is how we participate in others finding and grabbing hold of saving faith.

What are some of the biggest obstacles that keep you from sharing your faith with others?

What are some words you would use to describe your experiences with evangelism?

Where do you have an opportunity this week to make yourself available to someone who may be working through or struggling with questions of faith?

WALKING IN Crazy Faith

Every blessing and promise and provision God brings to you through crazy faith is intended to advance his mission of saving faith for everyone on the earth. After all, what good are luxury cars and custom houses and designer sneakers for your kids without a lasting spiritual legacy of saving faith? What good is a high-powered job if those who work for you never learn how much God loves them? What good is a miraculous healing if you just keep living for yourself? What good is deliverance from addiction if you're not going to help others get free of those chains?

Remember these steps in the progression of crazy faith:

- We *accept* salvation through saving faith in Christ.
- We gain *access* to the Holy Spirit, our live-in guide to God's life in us.
- We take *action* in prayer and in real life to obey God's Word. Baby steps!
- We take *authority* over anything that stands in the way of God's will.
- We live in *abundance*, a pipeline of blessing to everyone around us.

Why do we walk in 𝕮𝖗𝖆𝖟𝖞 𝕱𝖆𝖎𝖙𝖍? So that every single person we touch with our lives can experience saving faith in Jesus Christ and begin his or her own progression of faith. 𝕮𝖗𝖆𝖟𝖞 𝕱𝖆𝖎𝖙𝖍 is like a wave: it just keeps coming . . . and coming . . . and coming.

Together in this study, we've walked through baby faith, maybe faith, waiting faith, wavy faith, lazy faith, fugazi faith, trading faith, stating faith, fading faith, and saving faith—all on our way to living in 𝕮𝖗𝖆𝖟𝖞 𝕱𝖆𝖎𝖙𝖍. But that's not the end! Once you begin to experience God's promise and provision for your family, your career, your neighborhood, your physical health, and so much more, and you begin to live in abundance and purpose in the wave of 𝕮𝖗𝖆𝖟𝖞 𝕱𝖆𝖎𝖙𝖍 . . . *don't stop.* Keep your foot on the gas. Make the choice to not be comfortable in what your 𝕮𝖗𝖆𝖟𝖞 𝕱𝖆𝖎𝖙𝖍 has produced *so far.* Be open to beginning the maybe, waiting, wavy, active, declarative process all over again, full of trust for what your 𝕮𝖗𝖆𝖟𝖞 𝕱𝖆𝖎𝖙𝖍 *can still* produce.

Let me close with this prayer from the apostle Paul:

Now to him who is able to do immeasurably more than all we ask or imagine, according to his power that is at work within us, to him be glory in the church and in Christ Jesus throughout all generations, for ever and ever! Amen.

EPHESIANS 3:20-21

Welcome to your new normal. This is how it's supposed to be! God isn't interested in blessing you once; he is intent on opening his floodgates to pour down continually, confirming again and again for people ready to abandon hope that *he is real.*

So, when they all say it's impossible, when the calculations are improbable, and when everything looks just plain crazy . . . you look them straight in the eye, with your head up and shoulders back, and declare this: "It's only crazy until it happens."[12]

What has faith unlocked or accomplished in your life so far?

Where are you currently facing a choice to stay comfortable in what you've already been given or press forward toward something new?

What does it look like for you to *not* take your foot off the gas right now? What can you do this week to press down on that pedal?

Next Steps: Well done! You've been on a journey that took you all the way from baby faith to saving faith. As a next step, if you haven't already done so, you may want to read 𝕮𝖗𝖆𝖟𝖞 𝕱𝖆𝖎𝖙𝖍 from start to finish. Above all, continue to pursue **crazy faith** by spending time in God's Word and by engaging with other believers who are actively pursuing life with God.

LEADER'S GUIDE

Thank you for your willingness to lead your group through this study! What you have chosen to do is valuable and will make a great difference in the lives of others. The rewards of being a leader are different from those of participating, and we hope that as you lead you will find your own ℭraʒy ℱaith journey with Jesus deepened by this experience.

ℭraʒy ℱaith is a five-session Bible study built around video content and small-group interaction. As the group leader, imagine yourself as the host of a party. Your job is to take care of your guests by managing the behind-the-scenes details so that when your guests arrive, they can focus on one another and on the interaction around the topic for that session.

Your role as the group leader is not to answer all the questions or reteach the content—the video, book, and study guide will do most of that work fo you. Rather, your job is to guide the experience and cultivate your small group into a connected and engaged community. This will make it a place for members to process, question, and reflect—not necessarily receive more instruction.

There are several elements in this leader's guide that will help you as you structure your study and reflection time, so be sure to follow along and take advantage of each one.

BEFORE YOU BEGIN

Before your first meeting, make sure the group members have a copy of this study guide. Alternately, you can hand out the study guides at your first meeting and give the members some time to look over the material and ask any preliminary questions. Also make sure they are aware that they have access to the streaming videos at any time by following the instructions printed on the inside front cover. During your first meeting, ask the members to provide their name, phone number, and email address so you can keep in touch with them.

Generally, the ideal size for a group is eight to ten people, which will ensure that everyone has enough time to participate in discussions. If you have more people, you might want to break up the main group into smaller subgroups. Encourage those who show up at the first meeting to commit to attending the duration of the study, as this will help the group members get to know one another, create stability for the group, and help you know how to best prepare to lead them through the material.

Each of the sessions begins with an opening reflection in the "Welcome" section. The questions that follow in the "Share" section serve as an icebreaker to get the group members thinking about the topic at hand. Some people may want to tell a long story in response to one of these questions, but the goal is to keep the answers brief. Ideally, you want everyone in the group to get a chance to answer, so try to keep the responses to a minute or less. If you have talkative group members, say up front that everyone needs to limit their answer to one minute.

Give the group members a chance to answer, but also tell them to feel free to pass if they wish. With the rest of the study, it's generally not a good idea to have everyone answer every question—a free-flowing discussion is more desirable. But with the opening icebreaker questions, you can go around the circle. Encourage shy people to share, but don't force them.

At your first meeting, let the group members know each session contains a personal study section they can use to continue to engage with the content until the next meeting. While this is an optional exercise, it will help the members cement the concepts presented during the group study time and help them build their crazy faith by spending time in God's Word. Let them know that if they choose to do so, they can watch the video for the next session by accessing the streaming code found on the inside front cover of their studies. Invite them to bring any questions and insights they uncovered while reading to your next meeting, especially if they had a breakthrough moment or didn't understand something.

PREPARATION FOR EACH SESSION

As the leader, there are a few things you should do to prepare for each meeting:

- *Read through the session.* This will help you to become more familiar with the content and know how to structure the discussion times.

- *Decide how the videos will be used.* Determine whether you want the members to watch the videos ahead of time (via the streaming access code found on the inside front cover) or together as a group.

- *Decide which questions you want to discuss.* Based on the amount and length of group discussion, you may not be able to get through all the questions, so choose four to five that you definitely want to cover.

- *Be familiar with the questions you want to discuss.* When the group meets, you'll be watching the clock, so you want to make sure you are familiar with the questions you have selected. In this way, you'll ensure you have the material more deeply in your mind than your group members.

- *Pray for your group.* Pray for your group members and ask God to lead them as they study his Word.

In many cases, there will be no one "right" answer to the question. Answers will vary, especially when the group members are being asked to share their personal experiences.

STRUCTURING THE DISCUSSION TIME

You will need to determine with your group members how long you want to meet so that you can plan your time accordingly. Generally, most groups like to meet for either ninety minutes or two hours, so you could use one of the schedules found on the following page.

As the group leader, it is up to you to keep track of the time and keep things on schedule. You might want to set a timer for each segment so both you and the group members know when your time is up. (There are some good phone apps for timers that play a gentle chime or other pleasant sound instead of a disruptive noise.)

Don't be concerned if the group members are quiet or slow to share. People are often quiet when they are pulling together their ideas, and this might be a new experience for them. Just ask a question and let it hang in the air until

SECTION	90 MINUTES	120 MINUTES
WELCOME (members arrive and get settled)	10 minutes	15 minutes
SHARE (discuss one or more of the opening questions for the session)	10 minutes	15 minutes
READ (discuss the questions based on the Scripture reading for the session)	10 minutes	15 minutes
WATCH (watch the teaching material together and take notes)	20 minutes	20 minutes
DISCUSS (discuss the Bible study questions you selected ahead of time)	30 minutes	40 minutes
RESPOND / PRAY (pray together as a group and dismiss)	10 minutes	15 minutes

someone shares. You can then say, "Thank you. What about others? What came to you when you watched that portion of the teaching?"

GROUP DYNAMICS

Leading a group through **Crazy Faith** will prove to be highly rewarding both to you and your group members. But you still may encounter challenges along the way! Discussions can get off track. Group members may not be sensitive to the needs and ideas of others. Some might worry they will be expected to talk about matters that make them feel awkward. Others may express comments that result in disagreements. To help ease this strain on you and the group, consider the following ground rules:

- When someone raises a question or comment that is off the main topic, suggest that you deal with it another time, or, if you feel led to go in that direction, let the group know you will be spending some time discussing it.

- If someone asks a question that you don't know how to answer, admit it and move on. At your discretion, feel free to invite group members to comment on questions that call for personal experience.

- If you find one or two people are dominating the discussion time, direct a few questions to others in the group. Outside the main group time, ask the more dominating members to help you draw out the quieter ones. Work to make them a part of the solution instead of part of the problem.

- When a disagreement occurs, encourage the group members to process the matter in love. Encourage those on opposite sides to restate what they heard the other side say about the matter, and then invite each side to evaluate if that perception is accurate. Lead the group in examining other Scriptures related to the topic and look for common ground.

When any of these issues arise, encourage your group members to follow these words from the Bible: "Love one another" (John 13:34), "If it is possible, as far as it depends on you, live at peace with everyone" (Romans 12:18), "Whatever is true . . . noble . . . right . . . if anything is excellent or praise-worthy—think about such things" (Philippians 4:8), and, "Be quick to listen, slow to speak and slow to become angry" (James 1:19). This will make your group time more rewarding and beneficial for everyone who attends.

Thank you again for taking the time to lead your group. You are making a difference in the lives of others and having an impact on their journey toward greater 𝕮𝖗𝖆𝖟𝖞 𝕱𝖆𝖎𝖙𝖍.

ENDNOTES

1. "James Webb Space Telescope," NASA (accessed February 8, 2022), https://webb.nasa.gov/content/about/orbit.html.
2. Elizabeth Howell, "NASA's James Webb Space Telescope Is Cooling Down for Its Next Trick: Observing the Universe," Space.com, February 6, 2022, https://www.space.com/james-webb-space-telescope-chief-scientist-update.
3. Adapted from Michael Todd, *Crazy Faith* (Colorado Springs: Waterbrook Multnomah, 2021), pp. 54–56.
4. "Events," World's Strongest Man (accessed February 9, 2022), https://www.theworldsstrongestman.com/events/.
5. "1984," History Central (accessed February 9, 2022), https://www.historycentral.com/20th/1984.html.
6. Adapted from Michael Todd, *Crazy Faith*, pp. 94–96.
7. "Woman Fined €1,200 for Causing Tour de France Pile-up," BBC, December 9, 2021, https://www.bbc.com/news/world-europe-59582145.
8. Michael Todd, *Crazy Faith*, pp. 119–121.
9. Maya Riser-Kositsky, "Education Statistics: Facts About American Schools," EducationWeek (updated January 7, 2022), https://www.edweek.org/leadership/education-statistics-facts-about-american-schools/2019/01.
10. Michael Todd, *Crazy Faith*, pp. 139–142.
11. Marilyn Berger, "Desmond Tutu, Whose Voice Helped Slay Apartheid, Dies at 90," *The New York Times*, December 26, 2021, https://www.nytimes.com/2021/12/26/world/africa/desmond-tutu-dead.html; "Opposition to Apartheid," Britannica, https://www.britannica.com/topic/apartheid/Opposition-to-apartheid; "10 Questions for Desmond Tutu," *TIME*, March 22, 2020, http://content.time.com/time/subscriber/article/0,33009,1971410-1,00.html.
12. Adapted from Michael Todd, *Crazy Faith*, pp. 205–207.

Did *Crazy Faith* move you?
Challenge you?
Motivate you?

Share your thoughts with Pastor Mike about how *Crazy Faith* inspired you at IAmMikeTodd.com/CrazyFaithStories

WATERBROOK

IAmMikeTodd.com/CrazyFaithStories

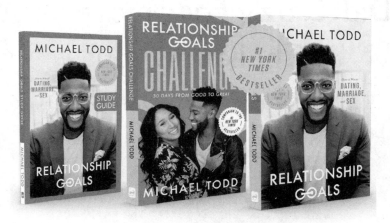

WHAT READERS ARE SAYING ABOUT *RELATIONSHIP GOALS*

"A great God-centered read."

"Chapters 8 and 9 are worth the buy . . ."

"A H.O.T. book (HONEST, OPEN, and TRANSPARENT)."

"Progress, not perfection."

"Get. This. Book."

WATERBROOK | IAmMikeTodd.com/Relationship-Goals

Also Available
from Michael Todd

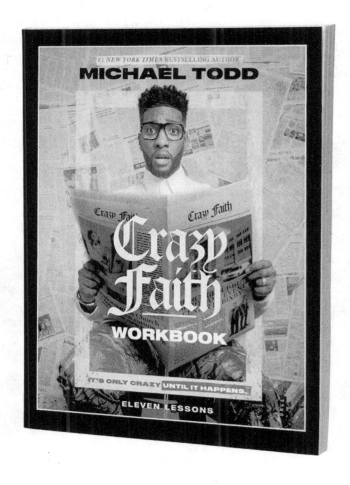

Available wherever books are sold.

Video Study for Your Church or Small Group

In this six-session study, Louie Giglio helps you apply the principles in *Don't Give the Enemy a Seat at Your Table* to your life. The study guide includes video notes, group discussion questions, and personal study materials for in between sessions.

Study Guide
9780310134244

DVD with
Free Streaming Access
9780310134268

Available now at your favorite bookstore,
or streaming video on StudyGateway.com.

Also Available
from Levi Lusko

Available now at your favorite bookstore,
or streaming video on StudyGateway.com.

Also Available
from Craig Groeschel

Available wherever books are sold.

We hope you enjoyed this Bible study from
HarperChristian Resources.

Find your next Bible study, video series, or ministry training at:
HarperChristianResources.com

YouTube.com/HarperChristianResources

Facebook.com/HarperChristianResources

Instagram.com/HarperChristianResources

Twitter.com/HCResources

—————— OUR MISSION ——————

Equipping people to understand the Scriptures, cultivate spiritual growth,
and live an inspired faith with Bible study and video resources
from today's most trusted voices.

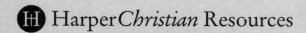